A Childlike Faith: A Collection of Christian Poems Written For God's Children of All Ages

Copyright © 2024 Teressa L Thomas

All rights reserved. No part of this book may be used or reproduced by any means, graphic, electronic, or mechanical, including photocopying, recording, taping or by any information storage retrieval system without the written permission of the author except in case of brief quotations embodied in critical articles and reviews.

Victory Publishing House Raleigh books may be ordered through booksellers or by contacting:

Victory Publishing House Raleigh
2825 S Wilmington St.
Raleigh, NC 27603
919-779-5180

Because of the dynamic nature of the internet, any web addresses or links contained in this book may have changed since publication and may no longer be valid. The views expressed in this work are solely those of the author and do not necessarily reflect the views of the publisher, and the publisher hereby disclaims any responsibility for them.

ISBN: 979-8-9903959-4-7 (sc)
ISBN: 979-8-9903959-5-4 (e)

Victory Publishing House Raleigh rev. date: 11/17/2025

A Childlike Faith

A Collection of Christian poems written for God's children of all ages

by Teressa L. Thomas

Table of Contents

Introduction: The Gift 10
The One...13
Without You..17
Incomparable..20
Watch Over Me..22
Walk With Me..24
The Path He Planned For Me..27
He is Here..30
Never Alone..32
You and Me...35
Christ in Me..38
The Greater One..40
The Answer to My Prayer..42
Blessings..44
Take a Closer Look...46
Can Not Be Cursed..49
The Eyes of Faith...52
What I Know..54
Thy Servant..56
Purpose and Provision..58
Be Still...60

Are You Listening?..62
Covid vs. Covered...65
Pandemic Pandemonium...69
The Truth of the Matter..73
Maggie..77
Calvin and Margie..81
Bluebird...85
His Way...88
About Time...91
My Card Box...94
The Fabric of Life...96
My Book...99
I Like Who I Am...104
Walk Ye In Him..107
He is Waiting..111
The Wedding Feast..114
The Pruning..116
In Our Weakness..118
There is More...120
Nothing More...123

Acknowledgements

I am most thankful to God for the precious gift of writing and for placing it back in my hand after I had wrapped it up and put it away. And for the beautiful way He revealed it to me. I am so thankful for the dreams, the words, His promptings, His encouragement, His voice, His wisdom, His direction, for opening doors, blocking roads, and for bringing help when I needed it. I am thankful to God for inspiring these poems and for the beautiful way that He touches people through them. I pray He will continue to do so.

I am thankful for the love, support, encouragement, and help of so many neighbors and friends over this six-year journey. Especially Genie Crooms, Stacey Lundy, Louise Harris, Pauline Goza and Ann Harper.

Special thanks to my brother Calvin and his wife Margie for their advice and for believing in me.

And to Isaiah Short for taking on the publishing of this book so that my vision would come to pass.

ALL GLORY TO GOD

"I know thy works: behold, I have set before thee an open door, and no man can shut it: for thou hast a little strength, and hast kept my word, and hast not denied my name." - Revelation 3:8

Introduction

The Gift
February 2024

I'm slowly opening a gift
That I wrapped up long ago.
Yet I knew nothing about it
'til my Father told me so.

He gave to me a dream one night
That was very vivid and swift.
I was standing in my foyer
And in my hand I held a gift.

I recognized this as a gift I had wrapped
Intending to give to someone.
Though I could not remember who or what
Or why that had not been done.

I started to unwrap this gift
To find out what was within.
But just as quickly as this dream had started
It abruptly came to an end.

Bright and early the next morning
As I was waiting for my coffee,
This odd little dream came back to mind
And its meaning was revealed to me.

He said "this is a gift intended for you
To give to others one day."
He said "it's your gift of writing
But you wrapped it up and put it away."

"Now I have placed it back in your hand"
This is a gift of great benefit.
"And where you started to open it up,
You've only begun to unwrap it."

That was several years ago
And this gift is so befitting.
This blessed gift from my Lord
Is a gift that will keep giving.

The One
January 2019

This poem is so special to me. It is like a fountain of love, based on the Word of God. When I read it to someone, even if we have just met, it takes us to another level. We become fused in the love of Christ. It breaks down walls and lets the pure love of God flow from one to another. It is such a beautiful reminder of the Father's love for us, a great encouragement for Christians, and a wonderful testimony for those seeking a relationship with the Lord. I give all glory to God for this poem.

For times past, present and yet to come, Jesus is the only one.

"The One I see without sight, the One I fear with fright."

"Greater love hath no man than this, that a man lay down his life for his friends." - John 15:13 KJV

"No man taketh it from me, but I lay it down of myself. I have power to lay it down, and I have power to take it again. This commandment I have received of my Father." - John 10:18 KJV

The One

The One from whom I cannot hide
The One who never leaves my side
The One who knew me before I was conceived
The One who rejoiced when first I believed
The One who knows my very heart
The One who stays and will not part
The One I love without cease
The One who brings me so much peace
The One who is my husband and friend
The One who loves me without end
The One I depend on for everything
The One who gives me songs to sing
The One and His righteousness I first seek
The One who hears me when I speak
The One whose inheritance is mine to share
The One my sin and sickness bear
The One who provides my every need
The One who multiplies my sown seed

The One who makes me without sin
The One who lives deep within
The One I need no ear to hear
The One who tells me "Do not fear"
The One that I so love and adore
The One that I know loves me more
The One who strengthens me when I take a stand
The One who upholds me with His righteous right hand
The One I see without sight
The One I fear without fright
The One who is my destiny
The One who gave His life for me
The One I trust, The One I seek
The One I find, The One so meek
The One on the cross, The One that won
The One said it is over for it has all been done

"Then spake Jesus again unto them, saying, I am the light of the world: he that followeth me shall not walk in darkness, but shall have the light of life." - John 8:12 KJV

Without You
June 6, 2022

"Then spake Jesus again unto them, saying, I am the light of the world: he that followeth me shall not walk in darkness, but shall have the light of life." - John 8:12 KJV

Without You

I would not even notice the sun without You,
Daylight could not bring things into view.

The songs of the birds would be just a waste,
Honey on my tongue would have no sweet taste.

The cumulus clouds that I love to see,
Would no longer be a delight to me.

A baby's laughter, the sweetest sound on earth,
Would not be as precious without my rebirth.

I could not truly know joy and peace,
No rest from worries, they would not cease.

The days would seem long as if without end,
A life without meaning I can't comprehend.

Father, without Your direction I would be lost,
I must be near to You at all cost.

Heavenly Father, I pray that those whom You draw
Will come running to You at Your beck and call.

When they've come to Christ and salvation is real,
They will begin understand how I must feel.

They'll see things differently, with great delight,
As they begin their walk in Your bright light.

Incomparable
February 13, 2021

"But thanks be to God, who always leads us in triumph in Christ, and through us spreads and makes evident everywhere the sweet fragrance of the knowledge of Him." - 2 Corinthians 2:14 AMP

"Be completely humble and gentle; be patient, bearing with one another in love." - Ephesians 4:2 NIV

Incomparable

Sitting in prayer I hear birds start to sing
Their beautiful morning melody
Yet it is not as beautiful as the sound that I hear
When my Lord speaks to me.

Walking outside on a lovely spring day
Smelling the flowers in bloom
Their perfume can't compare to the aroma that comes
When Glory enters into my room.

The celebration and wedding for a match made in heaven
Everything is so perfect and nice
But most beautiful of all is the love that is given
From one to another through Christ.

The worldly put value on power and wealth
To them fame and fortune is key
But I would not want it, it does not compare
To the blessings that God gives to me.

For serving others and doing God's will
I desire no accolades
I'll have my reward when I get to heaven
and meet Jesus face to face.

Watch Over Me
January 2019

"For God, who commanded the light to shine out of the darkness, hath shined in our hearts, to give the light of the knowledge of the glory of God in the face of Jesus Christ." - 2 Corinthians 4:6 KJV

"Pray ye therefore the Lord of the harvest, that he will send forth labourers into his harvest." - Matthew 9:38 KJV

"I laid me down and slept; I awaked; for the Lord sustained me." - Psalm 3:5 KJV

Watch Over Me

Please sustain me Lord I pray,
See me through another day.
Help me to see You in all creation,
That I may show greater appreciation.

May I see You shine in all Your people,
Like a cross of gold on a sunlit steeple.
Living for You and walking upright,
Like beacons showing the way to Christ.

Laboring for you all through the day,
Seeking to help those whom I may.
Not taking for granted that You are near,
But living in Your presence with reverential fear.

Then after following as You have led,
I will lay me down upon my bed.
Trusting You for the rest I need,
While You and Your angels watch over me.

Walk With Me
September 19, 2021

"Though I walk in the midst of trouble, thou wilt revive me: thou shalt stretch forth thine hand against the wrath of mine enemies, and thy right hand shall save me." - Psalm 138:7 KJV

"He shall cover thee with his feathers, and under his wings shalt thou trust: his truth shall be thy shield and buckler."
- Psalm 91:4 KJV

Walk With me

Walk with Me My child
I'll bring you through this day
Be not afraid of anything
I heard my Saviour say

Don't let the noise of the world
Cause you to want to stray
Covered by Me, under My feathers
Is right where you should stay

I can't make you remain
You do have your own will
But I will calm the storm
And pull you up the hill

Other voices call you
To listen is a bad choice
Let their screaming and shouting
Be drowned out by My still small voice

Listen to My direction
Walk with Me My friend
I will lead and make smooth your paths
From now until the end.

"Behold, I give unto you power to tread on serpents and scorpions, and over all the power of the enemy: and nothing shall by any means hurt you." - Luke 10:19 KJV

The Path He Planned For Me
October 1, 2019

"Show me the path where I should go, O Lord; point out the right road for me to walk." - Psalm 25:4 TLB

"Whether you turn to the right or to the left, your ears will hear a voice behind you, saying, 'This is the way; walk in it.'"
- Isaiah 30:21 NIV

"My sheep hear my voice, and I know them, and they follow me."
- John 10:27 KJV

The Path He Planned For Me

I'm right where I'm supposed to be
but this is not where I'll stay.
The Holy Spirit leads me further
down my path each day.

I pray to God and He points out
The way that I should go.
Then I head down my path He planned
with many seeds to sow.

When the road is somewhat foggy
or the path is not so smooth,
I hold tightly to His hand
and wait for Him to move.

I don't know where I'm going
but, oh, the places I have been.
He takes me where I've never gone
and never will again.

No one else can walk my path
He designed it just for me.
Everyone has their own path
God planned specifically.

If you are doubtful or uncertain
about what you should do,
Just ask the Lord to reveal
the path He planned for you.

What a glorious trail of seeds
I've been blessed to sow.
And oh, the many lovely people
I have come to know.

I can't see in the future
but what wonderful sights I see,
While walking with my Lord
down the path He planned for me.

He is Here
2019

The Lord gave me this poem one morning when I was in a place that made me feel a little uncomfortable. Not a bad place, but just a bit outside of my comfort zone. I have recited this poem many times in such situations. It always brings immediate peace.

"God did this so that they would seek him and perhaps reach out for him and find him, though he is not far from any one of us."
- Acts 17:27 NIV

He is Here

Where I am, He is here.
Ever present, ever near.
Anywhere, never fear.
For where I am,
He is here.

Never Alone
July 23, 2023

"Be strong and of a good courage, fear not, nor be afraid of them: for the Lord thy God, he it is that doth go with thee; he will not fail thee, nor forsake thee."
- Deuteronomy 31:6 KJV

"For we walk by faith, not by sight." - 2 Corinthians 5:7 KJV

Never Alone

People who know me, know I stay busy.
They know my spare minutes are few.
My time is spent on work and chores,
Instead of things I might like to do.

So not many stop by to visit,
And very few call on the phone.
I'm hardly ever invited out,
But that doesn't mean I'm alone.

I am so thankful for precious Jesus;
I've grown so much closer to Him.
He never leaves me – not for a minute,
He has become my best friend.

It may look like I'm by myself,
Anywhere I go.
But looks really are deceiving,
For where I go God goes.

So your eyes may see me all alone,
But it's the spirit world you can't see.
For there I hold the hand of God,
And He is leading me.

"I can do all things through Christ which strengtheneth me."
- Philippians 4:13 KJV

You and Me
October 3, 2020

"Having predestinated us unto the adoption of children by Jesus Christ to himself, according to the good pleasure of his will."
- Ephesians 1:5 KJV

"My substance was not hid from thee, when I was made in secret, and curiously wrought in the lowest parts of the earth. Thine eyes did see my substance, yet being unperfect; and in thy book all my members were written, which in continuance were fashioned, when as yet there was none of them." - Psalm 139:15-16 KJV

"For this God is our God for ever and ever; he will be our guide even to the end." - Psalm 48:14 NIV

You and Me

When I was not, You created me.
As I grew in the womb, You watched me.
Before I was born, You knew me.
When I did not know You, You called me.
When I was sad, You comforted me.
When I cried, You pacified me.
When danger was all around, You hid me.
When I felt I was alone, You surrounded me.
When it seemed I was invisible, You saw me.
When I thought I'd been forgotten, You remembered me.
When I was in the dark, You were light for me.
When I was unlovable, You loved me.
When I was headed the wrong way, You came after me.
When I would not see, You led me.
When I was proud, You broke me.
When I called out, You answered me.
When I accepted Christ, You adopted me.
When I came to You, You welcomed me.
When I hungered for truth, You fed me.
When I was weak, You strengthened me.
When I was wrong, You corrected me.
When I was sick, You healed me.

When I needed You, You enveloped me.
When I sought You, You came to me.
When I was uncertain, You guided me.
When I knowingly sinned, You convicted me.
When I repented, You forgave me.
When I was in need, You provided for me.
When storms came, You sheltered me.
When evil was near, You delivered me.
When deception crept in, You prayed for me.
When I was afraid, You went before me.
When I trusted You, You covered me.
When I humbled myself, You raised me.
When I thought I didn't matter,
You used me.

Father God what I know from all of my past
Is that You have always been with me
And from now and throughout eternity
You are and forever will be.

In the name of Jesus, I praise You.

Christ in Me
October 3, 2019

"Or which one of you, if his son asks him for bread, will give him a stone? Or if he asks for a fish, will give him a serpent? If you then, who are evil, know how to give good gifts to your children, how much more will your Father who is in heaven give good things to those who ask him!" - Matthew 7: 9-11 ESV

"I have been crucified with Christ. It is no longer I who live, but Christ who lives in me. And the life I now live in the flesh I live by faith in the Son of God, who loved me and gave himself for me."
- Galatians 2:20 ESV

"So let us come boldly to the throne of our gracious God. There we will receive his mercy, and we will find grace to help us when we most need it." - Hebrews 4:16 NLT

"To them God has chosen to make known among the Gentiles the glorious riches of this mystery, which is Christ in you, the hope of glory." - Colossians 1:27 NIV

Christ in Me

We live inside a balance
of our faith and His grace
He lives inside of those who ask
- those who seek His face.

Have confidence and faith in Him
His word always holds true
Just ask Him for He wants to come
and live inside of you.

You'll know then what you ought not do
by His Spirit that dwells within
A Light kept alive inside of you
and a deadness unto sin.

My sins have been forgiven
I approach Him without shame
I am honored He allows me
just to praise His Holy Name.

He fills my days with sunshine
He is the light that lets me see
He's my hope of glory
and He lives inside of me.

The Greater One
April 2022

"Ye are of God, little children, and have overcome them: because greater is he that is in you, than he that is in the world."
- 1 John 4:4 KJV

The Greater One

How cunning and wiling, so utterly beguiling
Satan's M.O. is most always deceit.
With words so witty, he'll prey on your pity
Don't let him become your defeat.

Charm hard to withstand, Satan wants to upend
Every good thing in life that you do.
But in you is Christ the Greater One
And He'll give the devil his due.

The Answer to My Prayer
August 2019

"I sought the Lord, and he heard me, and delivered me from all my fears." - Psalm 34:4 KJV

"O taste and see that the Lord is good: blessed is the man that trusteth in him." - Psalm 34:8 KJV

"Wait on the Lord: be of good courage, and he shall strengthen thine heart: wait, I say, on the Lord." - Psalm 27:14 KJV

"The righteous cry, and the Lord heareth, and delivereth them out of all their troubles." - Psalm 34:17 KJV

The Answer to My Prayer

I asked my Lord to help me, as I most humbly prayed,
For problems were abounding, and I was becoming afraid.

Provide for me all that I need, help me in all that I do,
I am but a tender reed, my all depends on You.

Oh Lord, I need many answers, wisdom at the least.
I cannot let my joy continue to be Satan's feast.

I reminded Him of His promises, I put Him to the test.
He said just watch Me work, while you be still and rest.

Then I felt an ease, as of a burden lifted,
To trust and continue waiting, was the answer my Lord gifted.

It's coming, yes it's coming; my help is on the way.
I'll just keep on waiting, it will be most any day.

Blessings
January 12, 2020

"For I know the plans I have for you", declares the Lord, "plans to prosper you and not to harm you, plans to give you hope and a future." - Jeremiah 29:11 NIV

"For the eyes of the Lord run to and fro throughout the whole earth, to shew himself strong in the behalf of them whose heart is perfect toward him." - II Chronicles 16:9a KJV

"For since the world began, no ear has heard, and no eye has seen a God like you, who works for those who wait on Him." - Isaiah 64:4 NLT

"You both precede and follow me. You place your hand of blessing on my head." - Psalm 139:5 NLT

Blessings

I wish that I could make you see
All the ways the Lord is blessing me.

You look at the way that I must live
As having very little to give.

You view me through the eyes of the world
And say "Pity on this poor girl."

What you see is my house falling apart;
God looks and sees a beautiful heart.

To you it looks like I struggle and wrestle;
My God sees me as a willing vessel.

I know I appear to be very poor
But my Father has told me "Soon, no more."

God has His hand upon things that I do,
He's given me a dream that will soon come true.

God knows the plans He has for me,
To bring me peace and prosperity,

Yes, He has given me a task to do
That one day may change your point of view.

Then your words will be congratulatory
And I will still say, "To God be the glory."

Take a Closer Look
June 29, 2023

"While we look not at the things which are seen, but at the things which are not seen: for the things which are seen are temporal; but the things which are not seen are eternal." - 2 Corinthians 4:18 KJV

"I will praise thee; for I am fearfully and wonderfully made: marvellous are thy works; and that my soul knoweth right well."
- Psalm 139:14 KJV

Take a Closer Look

You enter the room seeming unaware
That I am even standing here.
But I know in truth you had to see me
In order to ignore me so completely.

You brush me off not liking what you see
When you should really make the effort to get to know me.
You see colors, shapes, sizes and clothes.
But I am so much more than any of those.

Your eyes tell your mind what I am about
But God created me from the inside out.
I am much, much deeper than clothes and skin
My identity is not on the outside, but within.

I soar far above any cloud in the sky
No, you won't see the real me by looking through your eye.
So don't judge me by what your eyes think you see
I am a child of God! That's my identity.

"God is our refuge and strength, a very present help in trouble."
- Psalm 46:1 KJV

Cannot Be Cursed
October 16, 2021

"So shall my word be that goeth forth out of my mouth: it shall not return unto me void, but it shall accomplish that which I please, and it shall prosper in the thing whereto I sent it." - Isaiah 55:11 KJV

"My sheep hear my voice, and I know them and they follow me: and I give unto them eternal life, and they shall never perish, neither shall any man pluck them out of my hand." - John 10:27-28 KJV

"How shall I curse, whom God hath not cursed? Or how shall I defy, whom the Lord hath not defied?" - Numbers 23:8 KJV

Cannot Be Cursed

Father, what is wrong here?
Seems things have gone from bad to worse.
One would think I am wicked,
Or possibly under a curse.

I feel I am always under attack,
Father tell me what I should do.
In expectation I await your help,
My trust and confidence is in You.

Jesus is the Good Shepherd,
Watching, He is always near.
I stand on the promises of His Word,
I will not live in fear.

My faith in the Lord is strong,
In Him I find deep peace.
Standing amid so much wrong,
He makes my joy increase.

The Word of God cannot fail,
And His love is measureless.
His Word will not return to Him void,
So great is His faithfulness.

Yes, He is always guarding,
Never, ever does He sleep.
Every minute without departing,
He watches over His sheep.

Praise the Father, seek Him in earnest
You will feel your troubles reverse.
Those whom the Lord God has blessed,
Cannot ever be cursed.

The Eyes of Faith
November 2020

"For we walk by faith not by sight." - 2 Corinthians 5:7 KJV

*"For we live by believing and not by seeing."
- 2 Corinthians 5:7 NLT*

"Now faith is the substance of things hoped for, the evidence of things not seen." - Hebrews 11:1 KJV

The Eyes of Faith

My eyes see me limping in pain,
My faith shows me dancing again.

My eyes see me being put down,
My faith shows me wearing a crown.

My eyes see me with little to give,
My faith shows me helping people to live.

My eyes see me failing again,
My faith shows me victorious in Him.

My eyes see me bound and confined,
My faith shows me the victory is mine.

My eyes see me always outdone,
My faith shows me what Jesus has done.

My eyes see me being left out,
My faith shows me never without.

My eyes show me scared to pieces,
My faith shows me at peace with Jesus.

My eyes see me feeling worthless and lost,
My faith shows my price Jesus paid on the Cross.

What I Know
2022

"The Lord himself watches over you! The Lord stands beside you as your protective shade." - Psalm 121.5 NLT

"The Lord keeps you from all evil and preserves your life."
- Psalm 121:7 NLT

"He that dwelleth in the secret place of the most High shall abide under the shadow of the Almighty. I will say of the Lord, He is my refuge and my fortress: my God; in him will I trust."
- Psalm 91:1-2 KJV

What I Know

Is that my God is for me
Who can be against me
I know my God will provide all I need
It will be sufficient and overflowing
I know my God will protect me always
He keeps me from all evil

My confidence in what I know
Is because of who I know

My Lord, my Savior, my Teacher, my Light
My Friend, my Defender, my Strength
My Peace, my Portion, my Joy
My Healer, my Redeemer
Jesus, MY ALMIGHTY GOD

He is my refuge and my fortress
He is where I go
He is where I live

Thy Servant
August 9, 2020

"And take the helmet of salvation, and the sword of the Spirit, which is the word of God." - Ephesians 6:17 KJV

"His Lord said unto him, Well done, good and faithful servant; thou hast been faithful over a few things, I will make thee ruler over many things: enter thou into the joy of thy lord."
- Matthew 25:23 KJV

Thy Servant

Father I know You have a purpose for me
Please reveal it, if You will.
Open my eyes that I may see,
For Your desire I wish to fulfill.

Many twists and turns in my life
Are preparing me for this event.
Some things in my life that have seemed so wrong,
May have actually been heaven sent.

Whatever I need to get it done,
I know You will provide it all.
It is my heart to glorify You,
Please help me to know my call.

In Your time I will know,
And You will put me in position.
I will trust in You and battle on,
With your Word as my ammunition.

And on the day that I stand before You,
If I have been diligent and fervent.
My greatest desire is to hear You say,
"Well done, good and faithful servant."

Purpose and Provision
April 2023

"What then shall we say brothers and sisters? When you come together, each of you has a hymn, or a word of instruction, a revelation, a tongue or an interpretation. Everything must be done so that the church may be built up." - 1 Corinthians 14:26 NIV

"Then Peter opened his mouth, and said, Of a truth I perceive that God is no respecter of persons." - Acts 10:34 KJV

Purpose and Provision

God is no respecter of persons
No one is better than anyone
Anything I have been blessed to do
Is because of what Jesus has done

God has put in us all a gift
Something to give to others
In the body of Christ we are to share
What we have with our sisters and brothers

The Lord knows best, and what He gives
Is not at all our decision
He gives to each a special talent
That comes with purpose and provision

After many years I've finally learned
What the Lord has blessed me to do
In God's time He will reveal
The gift that He has for you.

Be Still
February 15, 2020

"Be still, and know that I am God: I will be exalted among the heathen, I will be exalted in the earth." - Psalm 46:10 KJV

"Cause me to hear thy loving kindness in the morning; for in thee do I trust: cause me to know the way wherein I should walk; for I lift up my soul unto thee." - Psalm 143:8 KJV

"In the morning, Lord, you hear my voice; in the morning I lay my requests before you and wait expectantly." - Psalm 5:3 NIV

Be Still

Here I sit in stillness waiting and longing to hear
The perfect Word from Jesus whispered in my heart's ear

I need this Word before I leave to get me through the day
I cannot leave without it, please tell me Lord I pray

This Word will be encouraging, it will be a guiding light
This Word will give me everything to last the day and night

This sweet Word from my Savior spoken while I am still
To me will be a treasure to help me do His will

A Word from Him I must have to go into the world
Where evil, sin, and mass confusion all will be unfurled

With patience I must wait for what He will reveal
The Word that my Lord gives will build faith and restore zeal

I will listen quietly—in stillness is my strength
I won't concern myself with noise nor with time's length

Once I get this Word, I'll have all I need
With the faith of Christ in me built up—then I will proceed

And when tomorrow comes, I'll be right here again
Awaiting God's instructing Word
I will not leave 'til then.

Are You Listening?
2022

The Lord let me know as I was writing this poem that we are like wind chimes and the Holy Spirit is like the wind, because He is what moves us.

"The wind blows wherever it pleases. You hear its sound, but you cannot tell where it comes from or where it is going. So it is with everyone born of the Spirit." - John 3:8 NIV

"Brethren, I count not myself to have apprehended: but this one thing I do, forgetting those things which are behind, and reaching forth unto those things which are before, I press toward the mark for the prize of the high calling of God in Christ Jesus."
- Philippians 3:13-14 KJV

"Delight thyself also in the Lord; and he shall give thee the desires of thine heart." - Psalm 37:4 KJV

Are You Listening?

I awake in the morning to the sound of a song
Still ringing in my ears
It is not meant for anyone else
Only for me to hear

On a warm summer day I am caressed
By a cool breeze fanned down from a tree
A peaceful smile forms across my face
God is speaking to me

The tones of the chimes are carried along
By the wind that made them ring
So sweet to my ears, I wish you could hear
Are you listening?

From a seed in the earth a sprout presses through
Just to get to the light
God is telling me as I press on through the dark
In Him I will be alright

These things to you may not sound like much
But to me pure joy they impart
I delight in the Lord and He speaks to me
With the desires of my heart

"Therefore I say unto you, What things soever ye desire, when ye pray, believe that ye receive them, and ye shall have them."
- Mark 11:24 KJV

Covid vs. Covered
March 24, 2020

"But seek ye first the kingdom of God, and his righteousness; and all these things shall be added unto you." - Matthew 6:33 KJV

"For God hath not given us the spirit of fear; but of power, and of love, and of a sound mind." - 2 Timothy 1:7 KJV

"Give all your worries and cares to God, for he cares about what happens to you." - 1 Peter 5:7 NLT

Covid vs. Covered

My God is more powerful than this disease
They call COVID-19
To rest in my Lord and stay in His Word
Is my place of quarantine.

People are mass buying and hoarding
All coming from fear and greed
Seek God first and His righteousness
And He will supply all you need.

I have no fear of this disease
My body is the Lord's temple
I am His child and I truly believe
It really is that simple.

God is my fortress, I will not fear
I dwell in a secret place
He has given His angels charge over me
To keep me in all of my ways.

I have not been given the spirit of fear
Read 2nd Timothy 1:7 to find
I have been given power and love
He has given me a sound mind.

I wear the armor found in Ephesians
Provided by my Lord
Truth, Righteousness, Peace, Faith, Salvation
And the Sword of His Word.

No, this dreaded disease cannot overcome me
I am saved through faith in Christ
It may take the breath from my body
but it can never take my life.

I have faith in the Word of God
I know His Word will not fail
I find strength in His Word and the power of His Might
Yes, I know my God will prevail.

He's a good Father, He loves us so much
And He wants for us what is best
Psalm 55:22 says give Him your worries
Now go get some rest.

"I have set the Lord always before me: because he is at my right hand, I shall not be moved." - Psalm 16:8 KJV

Pandemic Pandemonium
April 2020

"If my people, which are called by my name, will humble themselves, and pray, and seek my face, and turn from their wicked ways; then I will hear from heaven, and will forgive their sin, and will heal their land." - 2 Chronicles 7:14 KJV

Pandemic Pandemonium

I can't go to work now,
The business is shut down.
Can't eat in a restaurant,
No night on the town.

I can't go to a movie,
Can't go to a gym,
Can't go to the mall,
Can't go for a swim.

I can't go to church,
Can't be in a crowd.
Because of a coronavirus,
It is just not allowed.

So many restrictions
Causing an uproarious flop.
But what I desire most
The government can't stop.

I will seek and praise God
And hold tightly to His hand.
I'll pray for His protection
All across the land.

He always brings me comfort
He always gives me peace.
Worshipping Him with praise and song
Puts my mind at ease.

So I don't need a movie,
And I don't need a mall.
What I do need is Jesus
And He's always available to all.

"For I the Lord thy God will hold thy right hand, saying unto thee, Fear not; I will help thee." - Isaiah 41:13 KJV

The Truth of the Matter
July 14, 2024

"Be not deceived; God is not mocked: for whatsoever a man soweth, that shall he also reap." - Galatians 6:7 KJV

"Heaven and earth shall pass away, but my words shall not pass away." - Matthew 24:35 KJV

The Truth of the Matter

The lies spewing forth through the lips
Of those who are pointing their fingertips
At the righteous and just that walk upright
Continuous chatter that does not matter, right?
It's noise

Laughing and mocking, jeering and sneering
Babies are slaughtered, I can hear cheering
As children of God are being bound
There again I hear the ugly sound
Of noise

Is the media denied the freedom of speech?
Who is controlling the words they speak?
Relinquishing this freedom is self-abusing
Their reports are opinionated and confusing
All noise

To hear the sounds coming through my radio
I think would cause me to go below
What is this cacophony coming toward my ear
TURN IT OFF!!! There is nothing here to hear
It's noise

Politicians shout lies over opponents, what a racket
Yet each stands poised, ready to attack it
With a voice of arrogance they confidently shout
Don't fall victim to all they tout
It's just noise

What the government has caused this nation to become
Politically correct, we are silent and numb
My friend this is evil personified
A deafening silence that can't be denied
Still noise

Stay away from the things that promote fear
Incline your ear to what you should hear
Be receptive to the still small voice
What the Lord speaks forth is not noise
It's TRUTH!

Maggie
2020

In this poem about my little dog Maggie, look closely at her picture. I took this picture when she was probably just a year old. Notice how her eyes are totally focused on me and she has an ear raised, waiting to hear me speak. I am her master. Throughout this book you will see a depiction of Maggie's Ear, followed by a scripture. Where you see this, listen close and perk up your ear, just like Maggie did for me, intentionally listening to and meditating on these scriptures.

As she was toward me, reminded me, we should be toward the Lord -- and even more so.

"He keeps his eye upon you as you come and go and always guards you." - Psalm 121:8 TLB

"And ye shall seek me, and find me, when ye shall search for me with all your heart." - Jeremiah 29:13 KJV

Maggie

Maggie, I know you want to go out, but the sun has not come up
You'll have to wait until it's light. I'm sorry my little pup.
Maggie I like that you let me know all you want to do
But when I say "no" I hope you'll know it's out of my love for you
I want to grant you your desire, but the time is just not right.
I wish you could know that bringing you joy gives me great delight.
I can't let you out now to wander in darkness, there are dangers
you can't foresee.
Maggie girl, I know what's best; you'll have to wait on me.

I hear you loud and clear, my Lord, your message is coming through.
For these things I say to Maggie, I also hear from you.

Maggie can't find her frisbee. She's looking all around.
If she would just listen and come to me, it would be easily found.
She seems a little panicked. I wish she would obey.
It's lying on the path to me, and she'd find it along the way

Oh Father, I hear You speaking to me, as I want her to obey.
You beckon me come to You, and ask me not to stray.
The way for me will be so clear, and I'll find all I need.
If I incline my ear to hear, and my Master's voice I heed.

Maggie's leash is long and retractable, so I let her run on ahead.
But when I sense danger I pull her in close so she can be safely led.
Maggie doesn't know all that I know and she can't see all that I see.
I'm not even sure she is aware that she's always watched over by me.

Father You have given me free rein to do the things I like to do.
But when I feel Your tug I should heed, 'tis then best I draw close to You.
Precious Father, I am finally learning, that Your eyes are forever on me.
You lead me to walk in safety, and You protect me constantly.

Maggie likes being close to me, and lying at my feet.
But even if she's across the room, her eyes are fixed on me.
She will not look away, as if doing what she must.
With adoration she watches me through eyes of love and trust.
But if she gets tired, and her little eyes close, and if I should get up and leave.
When she awakens to find me gone, the first thing she'll do is seek me.

I'm reminded, Lord, I am most content, when I worship You.
May I keep You always in my heart, and forever in my view.

Maggie, through our many years, I've taught you quite a bit.
To heel and look, to take and put, to sing and stay and spit.
Many important things I have taught you that is true
But I find the greater value now is what I've learned through you.

"My Father, which gave them me, is greater than all; and no man is able to pluck them out of my Father's hand. I and my Father are one." - John 10:29-30 KJV

Calvin and Margie
October 2023

To understand this poem there are a few things you should know about my brother Calvin and his wife Margie:
- Before they met, Margie was looking for an apartment. She found the complex she wanted, but the Lord wouldn't let her take the first 2 apartments she looked at. He told her they were not right for her. Finally on the 3rd one, the Lord told her that was the one she should take. It turned out to be 1 apartment over from Calvin's apartment.
- While moving in it started to rain. She spotted Calvin and his friend and asked if they would help to move her piano quickly inside. She was afraid to ask Calvin at first because she was from the country, and "he was from the city."
- You should also know that Margie's nickname was "Squeal."
- They married in their home, but the county of their home and the county on the marriage certificate differed. So they had to drive across the county line, and on the roadside, they repeated their vows to make it legal.

"With all lowliness and meekness, with longsuffering, forbearing one another in love; endeavoring to keep the unity of the Spirit in the bond of peace." - Ephesians 4:2-3 KJV

"He shall not be afraid of evil tidings: his heart is fixed, trusting the Lord." - Psalm 112:7 KJV

"By this shall all men know that ye are my disciples, if ye have love one to another." - John 13:35 KJV

"I have told you this so that my joy may be in you and that your joy may be complete. My command is this: Love each other as I have loved you."
- John 15:11-12

"Let your light so shine before men, that they may see your good works, and glorify your Father which is in heaven."
- Matthew 5:16 KJV

Calvin and Margie

Years ago before their lives would start,
God sealed a marriage in a young couple's heart.

Calvin, a young man from the "big city world"
met pretty Nurse Margie, a sweet country girl.

Their meeting was exactly what God had in store
when He made Margie the girl next door.

Because of a piano and a little rain,
their lives would never again be the same.

Calvin knew in his heart he would marry "Squeal,"
as mentioned before it was already sealed.

Margie knew too but had to make known,
she would not be in a marriage without Christ in their home.

Calvin agreed, so Margie said "Yes."
From the very beginning this marriage was blessed.

They married in the presence of God, family and friends,
then crossed the county line and did it again.

Obstacles and hurdles they had to overcome.
They stood on God's Word knowing the battle was won.

Through trials and struggles their faith was not fazed.
They knew Christ would bring victory; they gave God praise.

Hard times and sad times were hardly any
when compared to the laughter and joys – so many.

Growing in love, becoming closer each day.
It didn't just happen, God made them that way.

Now Calvin has such a heart for the lost,
and Margie witnesses for their sake and cause.

With wisdom and testimony they now walk through life.
Spreading joy and laughter, sharing the love of Christ.

God was the one who joined them together,
and He creates marriages to last forever.

Calvin is now 70 and Margie 69.
Forty years into their marriage divine.

This poem for their 40th Anniversary is done.
As for Calvin and Margie... there is more yet to come.

Happy Anniversary to my precious brother and sister!   Love,
Teressa

"My sheep hear my voice, and I know them, and they follow me..."
- John 10:27 KJV

Bluebird
May 19, 2023

This poem was written for some of my dear neighbors after the death of their baby. His name was Theo, which means God's gift. Theo lived a little over 3 months. They planted a little garden in memory of Theo. One morning, while Theo's mother, grandmother and aunt were out for a walk, a little bluebird came hopping down the sidewalk toward them. They walked toward him and he kept hopping toward them until they finally stopped so they would not get too close and scare him away; he also stopped. They began speaking to him, and it seemed like he was listening, watching them and turning his head to the side. They thought of this little bird as a sign from their baby. While I know this bluebird was not their baby, I do believe the Lord sends messages in many ways. They have had many experiences with bluebirds since then.

I couldn't begin to comprehend, in any way, the pain they were going through, but I wanted to write something that would help bring them comfort. This poem was written from the mother's perspective out of great compassion for them.

"Then the Lord said to Elijah, "Go to the east and hide by Kerith Brook at a place east of where it enters the Jordan River. Drink from the brook and eat what the ravens bring you, for I have commanded them to bring you food." - 1 Kings 17:2-4 NLT

"After another 40 days, Noah opened the window that he had made in the boat and released a raven that flew back and forth until the earth was dry." - Genesis 8:6-7 NLT

"And the dove came in to him in the evening; and, lo, in her mouth was an olive leaf pluckt off: so Noah knew that the waters were abated from off the earth." - Genesis 8:11 KJV

"The Lord is close to the brokenhearted; he rescues those whose spirits are crushed." - Psalm 34:18 NLT

Bluebird

Little bluebird perched so near
Have you a song that I am to hear?
You fly to me from up in the sky
Dare I ponder the reason why?

So pretty you are in spectacular blue
How beautifully our Creator has clothed you.
Pretty bluebird that I'm blessed to see
Do you have a message for me?

You flit and flutter all around
You sit up high then dive to the ground
Playful, cheerful, what joy you bring
I await to hear the song you'll sing

Come sit inside the garden with me
We'll watch it grow to maturity
The plants and seeds have all been sown
Won't you watch with me 'til it's grown?

Stay with me a little while
Sweet bluebird how you make me smile
In the garden peace is thick
And the atmosphere is quite cathartic

Please sit with me a little longer
I'm feeling better and so much stronger
But little bluebird I know you can't stay
Your time has come to fly away

Watching with a tear in my eye
As you fly off into the evening sky
You leave me now but I pray
I'll see you again another day

In Psalm 34:18, it is written
That God is close to the brokenhearted.
And Matthew states that without the Father,
Not one sparrow has departed.

Theo's garden is representative
Of life's cycle in continuance
Sown seeds grow plants that produce more seeds
That in turn will produce more plants.

Lord, Theo is now nurtured in your arms
And your messengers, to his family, bring comfort.
It's the Light of Your Word and merciful care
That will heal their broken hearts.

His Way
April 16, 2023

"As for God, his way is perfect: The Lord's word is flawless; he shields all who take refuge in him." - Psalm 18:30 NIV

"Whoso mocketh the poor reproacheth his Maker: and he that is glad at calamities shall not be unpunished." - Proverbs 17:5 KJV

"Hearken, my beloved brethren, Hath not God chosen the poor of his world rich in faith, and heirs of the kingdom which he hath promised to them that love him?" - James 2:5 KJV

"So in everything, do to others what you would have them do to you, for this sums up the Law and the Prophets."
- Matthew 7:12 NIV

His Way

May your heart be always forgiving,
In the amount that you have received.
By Grace from your compassionate Father,
Through Jesus in whom you believe.

Always allow many chances
For those by whom you've been grieved.
They may not actually be bad people
They themselves may be deceived.

Never look down on the poor
Don't ever mock them in jest.
While they are lacking in worldly things,
Spiritually, they may be well blessed.

Don't treat some better than others
Just because they have obtained much wealth.
God commands us to love all our neighbors
As much as we love ourselves.

Do not seek to befriend people
Based on what they can do for you.
That's not the Lord's way and always remember
He knows and sees all you do.

Be forgiving, loving, kind and gentle
Praise the Lord and stay in His Word.
The greatest reward you will ever have
Is the blessing of knowing the Lord.

"For with God nothing shall be impossible." - *Luke 1:37 KJV*

About Time
May 2019

"And the second is like it: Love your neighbor as yourself."
- Matthew 22:39 NIV

"Do to others as you would have them do to you." - Luke 6:31 NIV

"For everything there is a season, and a time for every matter under heaven." - Ecclesiastes 3:1 ESV

About Time

When I rise to greet the day brand new,
I'm aware of time ticking away.
I begin to think of all I must do,
With just 24 hours in the day.

I rush to get here and push to get there,
Seems I struggle to be on time anywhere.
Bound by this burden I am beneath,
Arriving on time by the skin of my teeth.

I try to improve punctuality,
But I'm a slave to the clock – that's reality.
And the technology now to make things quick,
All for the clock's incessant tick.

Feeling always under attack,
A few more hours is all I lack.
Then at the sight of the setting sun,
I reflect on all that I have not done.

Not enough, not enough, not nearly enough,
But I must rest for the next day.
I look down at my wrist, a metal cuff,
Shows time still ticking away.

But wait just a minute – hold on a second!
I must change my point of view.
From all the things that I did not,
To that which I did do:

I took a quick moment to wave to a boy,
I praised my Lord and sang a song of joy.
I helped a baby bird back to its nest,
I trusted the Lord, and He gave me rest.
I gave encouragement to a neighbor passing by,
To a precious little baby, I sang a lullaby.
I took the time to smile at a stranger,
Watched children cross the street till safe from danger.
It took only minutes to look up scripture,
I saw a pretty flower and had to take a picture.
I brought a little dog that was out on his own,
To a family so grateful to have him back home.
I fed the neighbor's cat while she was away,
I called someone to say, "Happy Birthday."
Then I made time to call my oldest brother,
That meant I had to call the other.
I went to the store for a friend who was sick,
Now that took a few minutes cause I'm not very quick.
I listened as a senior told stories I had heard,
But intently, again, I took in each word.

So, I do believe I could be on time,
If I left all these little things out.
But to do so I fear would be unkind,
And not what life is about.
So, take notice of all that goes on around you,
Help out your neighbors and do all you can do.
See these small things they all add up,
To give me an overflowing cup.
So, a few minutes here and a few more there
To please my Lord sublime,
If it makes me late, I will not care
It only took time.

My Card Box
February 4, 2023

This was originally called Selma's Card Box. I wrote it for my friend Selma for her birthday. I gave her a pretty box with cards, stationery, a pen and stamps.

"Therefore encourage one another and build each other up, just as in fact you are doing." - 1 Thessalonians 5:11 NIV

My Card Box

I must sit down and write
To a family member or friend,
There is bound to be a special event
To use my paper and pen.

Maybe I'll send just a quick note
To let someone know they're thought about,
Maybe a card encouraging faith
In case they've begun to doubt.

I'll send someone a birthday card
I'll send someone a letter,
To someone I'll send a thank you note
For making my life better.

Anniversaries, a new home, a baby's birth
Get well, have a great vacation,
My box has quite an assortment
A card for every occasion.

I'll sit down with my pretty box
Containing all I need,
To let someone know they matter
And how special they are to me.

With careful consideration
My words written just for their need,
I'll smile thinking of how they will feel
As they open my letter and begin to read.

The Fabric of Life
January 2021

"And we know that in all things God works for the good of those who loveth him, who have been called according to his purpose."
- Romans 8:28 NIV

"Not forsaking the assembling of ourselves together, as the manner of some is; but exhorting one another: and so much the more, as ye see the day approaching." - Hebrews 10:25 KJV

The Fabric of Life

We all work together for God's purpose.
Like threads in fine linen we move toward each other
And cross one over the other, helping to hold each other up

We are drawn –
Some going east, some going west,
Some north, some south, over and under.
All through life we cross paths,
Weaving a beautiful, multi-patterned fabric.

It is in our gathering that the fabric is strengthened.
And from our love for one another through Christ
With this magnificent cloth,
He covers us.

"When thou saidst, Seek ye my face; my heart said unto thee, Thy face, Lord, will I seek." - Psalm 27:8 KJV

My Book
The Thick and Thin of It
December 27, 2023

"So then every one of us shall give account of himself to God."
- Romans 14:12 KJV

"Death and life are in the power of the tongue: and they that love it shall eat the fruit thereof." - Proverbs 18:21 KJV

"Jesus said unto him, I am the way, the truth, and the life: no man cometh unto the Father, but by me." - John 14:6 KJV

"For I will be merciful to their unrighteousness, and their sins and their iniquities will I remember no more." - Hebrews 8:12 KJV

My Book
The Thick and Thin of It

Father, You alone created me
You know my every thought and deed,
Recording them in a journal on me
That one day together we both will read.

I wonder what I would think
Of what is written in my book.
Suppose one day I had the chance
To quickly take a look.

Oh wow! There's my book...look how thick!!
God has really been watching me.
But thumbing through the pages
I don't like all that I see.

It contains the story of my life
From the first to the very last minute,
The good, the bad, the in-between
All are written down within it.

It shows the way I have lived
It lists all I have done,
It tells of all the life and death
I have spoken with my tongue.

The times I've spent with God
The times I've spent without,
The times I've trusted in Him
The times I've lived in doubt.

The ugly days of darkness
I hoped no one would see,
His light now shines brightly on pages
Of things I don't like about me.

The situations when I should have left
The ones when I should have stayed.
The times I was critical of others
When instead I should have prayed.

The "helpful" things I have done
When my motives were not pure,
The worry and anguish my actions
Caused others to endure.

The time someone needed my help
And I could have made a difference,
Instead I turned and walked away
I should have come to their defense.

I did not care about forgiving others
Or if I had been forgiven,
I did not know at that time
That Christ is the only way to heaven.

But then there's the time all alone
Sitting on the edge of my bed,
I gave my life over to Jesus
To be cleansed and Spirit led.

Now the pages once so full
Of sin have been wiped clean,
They are not remembered by God
In fact, they no longer will be seen.

And my book that once was so thick
Now is very thin,
The bad things have been removed
There is only good within.

Praying my book will again be thick
But this time filled with good deeds,
As I do my best to help care for others
I'll trust God to take care of me.

"Continue in prayer, and watch in the same with thanksgiving;"
- Colossians 4:2 KJV

I Like Who I Am
January 7, 2024

"And the peace of God, which passeth all understanding, shall keep your hearts and minds through Christ Jesus." - Philippians 4:7 KJV

I Like Who I Am

Thank You Father for this day
May I live it as You would have me.
And thank You for another day
To spend with my little dog Maggie.

Thank You God for a few more hours
To show others how much I care.
Thank You Father for blessing me
With a little extra to share.

Thank You for more time for me
To store up treasures in Heaven.
I praise You Father for growing me
Making me better than I've ever been.

Thank You for the wonderful joy
That comes from knowing You.
And thank You for the peace that comes
From knowing that You know me too.

Thank You Father for gently guiding me
As I go along my way.
Because of the changes You have made
I like who I am today.

"Let the words of my mouth, and the meditation of my heart, be acceptable in thy sight, O Lord, my strength, and my redeemer."
- Psalm 19:14 KJV

Walk Ye in Him
September 21, 2021

"As ye have therefore received Christ Jesus the Lord, so walk ye in Him." - Colossians 2:6 KJV

"Therefore if any man be in Christ, he is a new creature: old things are passed away; behold, all things are become new." - 2 Corinthians 5:17 KJV

"Whosoever abideth in him sinneth not: whosoever sinneth hath not seen him, neither known him." - 1 John 3:6 KJV

"For we know that our old self was crucified with him so that the body ruled by sin might be done away with, that we should no longer be slaves to sin – because anyone who has died has been set free from sin." - Romans 6:6-7 NIV

"Whoever abides in Him does not sin. Whoever sins has neither seen Him nor known Him." - 1 John 3:6 NKJV

Walk Ye in Him

So you say you are saved and have been for years,
But I tell you that's not what I see.
I see no fruit, I think you're lukewarm,
You're the same as you used to be.

There should be spiritual growth all along,
When the Holy Spirit dwells within.
The heart should no longer desire to do wrong,
There should be conviction of sin.

I don't like to judge, but I must say the truth,
Your actions speak louder than words.
Turn from your idols, there is but one Master,
The Lord God is who you should serve.

You've been to enough funerals that you can recite,
The 23rd Psalm by heart.
And almost sing Amazing Grace,
If you can remember how it starts.

Prayer is not just for early in the morning,
Nor just when you go to bed.
Don't let the prayer before your meal,
Be the only time you bow your head.

God is not just for weddings and funerals,
He's not just for Christmas and Easter.
He's not just for when someone is sick,
He's not just for good times either.

Christ is always speaking to you,
You need to take time to hear.
Christ is for anytime, all the time,
Every day of the year.

I hope I am wrong, but I fear that I see,
Someone still walking in sin.
Change your ways and repent, and if you are saved,
Then so walk ye in Him.

God put it in my heart to tell you this,
I'm just trying to open your eyes.
The best thing you will ever do,
Is to be totally focused on Christ.

You may think that I'm being harsh,
But it's better you find out now.
Start talking to Him, He will answer you,
Seek the Lord while He may be found.

"Humble yourselves in the sight of the Lord, and he shall lift you up." - James 4:10 KJV

He is Waiting
September 21, 2021

"But whoever drinks the water I give them will never thirst. Indeed, the water I give them will become in them a spring of water welling up to eternal life." - John 4:14 NIV

"For with the heart one believes unto righteousness, and with the mouth confession is made unto salvation." - Romans 10:10 NKJV

"For we do not have a high priest who is unable to empathize with our weaknesses, but we have one who has been tempted in every way, just as we are – yet he did not sin." - Hebrews 4:15 NIV

"Oh, taste and see that the Lord is good! Blessed is the man who trusteth in him!" - Psalm 34:8 KJV

"For whoever calls on the name of the Lord shall be saved." - Romans 10:13 NKJV

He is Waiting

Where do you find strength when you are weak
How do you find rest when you get none from sleep.

Do you feed your hunger and still feel hollow
Is your thirst so great that you can't even swallow.

Where do you go when you have no home
Do you really enjoy being alone?

The world looks at you and labels you useless
And your many bad choices offer no excuses.

The days are so long and the nights so black
All of your life you've been living in lack.

When you've had enough of a life filled with sin
Open your heart and let Jesus in.

With Christ you'll find sweet relief
Trading forgiveness for repentance and salvation for belief.

He will meet you anytime wherever you desire
He will wade through the flood, He will walk through the fire.

Don't be afraid! Take hold of His hand,
He wants to help you – He understands.

Forever in Him you will have all you need,
An abundant life and a sweet, deep peace.

He is good! Oh, taste and see,
When He sets you free, you are free indeed.

Call out His name with a heart that is true.
He's been watching. He's been waiting for you.

The Wedding Feast
August 23, 2023

"Let us be glad and rejoice, and give honour to him: for the marriage of the Lamb is come, and his wife hath made herself ready. And to her was granted that she should be arrayed in fine linen, clean and white: for the fine linen is the righteousness of the saints. And he saith unto me, Write, Blessed are they which are called unto the marriage supper of the Lamb. And he saith unto me, These are the true sayings of God." - The Revelation 19:7-9 KJV

The Wedding Feast

Come and join me, won't you?
I'm going to the table to eat.
At the bountiful wedding feast,
My Lord has prepared for me.

You must have received the invitation,
He sent it over and over again.
What a blessed gift to be invited!
You know, Christ is the only way in.

Down to the tiniest detail
God has watched over with care,
Even providing the wedding clothes
That everyone is to wear.

Surely you have a seat
Waiting at the table for you.
You did accept the invitation,
You will be there....won't you?

The Pruning
September 6, 2023

"I am the vine, and my Father is the gardener. He cuts off every branch of mine that doesn't produce fruit, and he prunes the branches that do bear fruit so they will produce even more." - John 15:1-2 NLT

"For everything there is a season, a time for every activity under heaven." - Ecclesiastes 3:1 NLT

The Pruning

I have been pruned by the hand of God
The part He removed was huge
But it had served its purpose
And no longer would be used

The wound is fresh, it is so very painful
And the cut goes in so deep
I humble myself before my God
And all I can do is weep

But my faith and trust in the Lord is great
All of my confidence is in Him
He knows best how to prepare me
For what is around the bend

I know this pruning will bring growth
And I will come out so much stronger
I will have to endure this pain and suffering
For only a short while longer

Scripture says there is a time, a season
For each thing under the sun
Sometimes it seems things are taken
When yet they have hardly begun

All of us experience the pain of loss
When a loved one is taken away
Though while in grief we are comforted to know
That our Lord will always stay

In Our Weakness
December 7, 2023

"For the mountains shall depart, and the hills be removed; but my kindness shall not depart from thee, neither shall the covenant of my peace be removed, saith the Lord that hath mercy on thee."
- Isaiah 54:10 KJV

"For as the heavens are higher than the earth, so are my ways higher than your ways and my thoughts than your thoughts."
- Isaiah 55:9 KJV

"These things I have spoken unto you, that in me ye might have peace. In the world ye shall have tribulation: but be of good cheer; I have overcome the world." - John 16:33 KJV

"And he said unto me, My grace is sufficient for thee: for my strength is made perfect in weakness. Most gladly therefore will I rather glory in my infirmities, that the power of Christ may rest upon me." - 2 Corinthians 12:9 KJV

In Our Weakness

Many things that happen in life
Tempt us to question why
Why did this happen to me?
Why did they have to die?

God's ways are higher than ours
Many times only He knows the reason
What we do not know right now
We may understand in due season

We are not promised an easy life
Jesus has made that clear
But in accepting Christ and trusting Him
He has promised to always be near

Problems will arise, don't be discouraged
For in Him we are truly blessed
We can call on the Lord to fight our battles
In our weakness His strength shows best

There is More
September 5, 2023

"The secret things belong unto the Lord our God: but those things which are revealed belong to us and to our children for ever, that we may do all the words of this law." - Deuteronomy 29:29 KJV

"Whereas ye know not what shall be on the morrow. For what is your life? It is even a vapour, that appeareth for a little time, and then vanisheth away." - James 4:14 KJV

"For the wages of sin is death; but the gift of God is eternal life through Jesus Christ our Lord." - Romans 6:23 KJV

There is More

How many more sunrises will I see,
How many are the days left for me?

The world spins on its axis I'm told;
How many more cycles will I behold?

How many more times will I walk in the moonlight,
Or hear the owl's call in the darkness of night?

How many more sunsets will I see,
How many until it sets on me?

I know that I am not promised tomorrow;
Time is not something that I can borrow.

Some things are known by God alone,
But I know after this life I will live on.

"And ye shall seek me, and find me, when ye shall search for me with all your heart." Jeremiah 29:13 KJV

Nothing More
June 16, 2024

"However, do not rejoice that the spirits submit to you, but rejoice that your names are written in heaven." - Luke 10:20 NIV

"Likewise the Spirit also helps in our weaknesses. For we do not know what we should pray for as we ought, but the Spirit Himself makes intercession for us with groanings which cannot be uttered."
- Romans 8:26 NKJV

"Blessed are those who wash their robes, so that they will have the right to the tree of life, and may enter the city by the gates."
- Revelation 22:14 NASB

Nothing More

As perfect as you
Perceive yourself to be
You're not good enough
To go to the cross for me

There is but one
Who holds that honor
Created in Heaven
And sent by the Father

Who else could pay such a great price,
Who alone is worthy.
Nothing more can be done to atone for sin,
Christ has done it perfectly.

Out of love and obedience He went to the cross,
And willingly He became my sacrifice.
He gave all He had to give for me,
To Him I'm the pearl of great price.

What more could I ever do,
I can't add to what Jesus has done.
Christ alone and nothing more
Has reserved my eternity in heaven.

Filled and sealed with His Holy Spirit
Who when I pray, intercedes.
That is God praying to God
---on behalf of me.

He is my great hope of hope
I have given Him all of me.
Secure in the perfection of His resurrection
There is nothing more I need.

Clothed in a robe that has been washed clean
By the powerful blood of the Lamb,
One day I will be able to stand at the Throne
In the presence of the great I AM

ABOUT THE AUTHOR

Teressa was born in Raleigh, NC and has lived there all of her life. At a very young age her love for poetry, music and nature was apparent and was encouraged by her parents. She had a talent for writing, especially poetry. In her late teens, for some reason, she began to distance herself from writing, though never losing her love for poetry. But in December of 2018, the Lord brought it back to her in a powerful way. Thus began the amazing journey of creating this book.

"I see the beauty of the Lord when I look deeply into the hearts of others. I am drawn to animals, clouds, trees, flowers and the rising and setting of the sun. I find the Lord all around me in the treasures He places in my path. The gentle lovingkindness of God along with these beautiful things inspire me to pour out my heart onto paper through my pen." TLT

www.ingramcontent.com/pod-product-compliance
Lightning Source LLC
Chambersburg PA
CBHW071119160426
43196CB00013B/2634